First Melodies

firstmelodies.com

Melody
Sings at the zoo

Written & Illustrated by Kirsty Clinch

This book belongs too

....

Dedicated to
Phil Glasson

Hello I'm Melody, I sing, dance and play.
I live in a land not too far away.
I go on adventures and have lots of fun,
and sing songs to everyone.
Today I am going to the zoo,
let's find the animals and learn something too.

Hello I'm Melody, how are you?
Who are you, and what do you do?
I sing, dance, play and learn every day.
I've come to the zoo,
to learn fun things about you.

The
Monkeys

Song

Look at me, I'm a monkey.
I like to climb up the trees.
I will not stop, till I get to the top
because I'm a cheeky monkey.

Look at me, I'm a monkey.
I like to swing on the trees.
I will not stop, till I swing to the top
because I'm a cheeky monkey.

Hello I'm Melody, how are you?
Who are you, and what do you do?
I sing, dance, play and learn every day.
I've come to the zoo,
to learn fun things about you.

The
Giraffes

Song

I'm Gina Giraffe and I jiggle and laugh.
Jiggle, jiggle, jiggle, jiggle.
Ha ha ha.
(Repeat x2)

My neck is long,
I am yellow and brown.
Have you ever seen a giraffe
jiggle and laugh?
(Repeat x2)

Hello I'm Melody, how are you?
Who are you, and what do you do?
I sing, dance, play and learn every day.
I've come to the zoo,
to learn fun things about you.

The
Elephants

Song

Elephants play the trumpet with their trunks.
(Repeat x2)
We play it when we're happy.
We play it when we're sad.
But we never forget how to play our
trumpets well.

Elephants play the trumpet with their trunks.
(Repeat x2)
We play it with excitement.
We play it when we're mad.
But we never forget how to play our
trumpets well.

Hello I'm Melody, how are you?
Who are you, and what do you do?
I sing, dance, play and learn every day.
I've come to the zoo,
to learn fun things about you.

The
Meerkats

Song

There's a meerkat here,
a meerkat there.
We stand with our bellies
in the air.
This is my Gang,
this is where we hang,
and I'm the sentry.

There's a meerkat here,
a meerkat there.
Have you seen us on telly?
We dress in clothes,
that was our goal,
and to keep healthy.

Song

I'm the king of the jungle
and I'm in town.
I walk around with my big shiny crown.
You will hear a ROAH,
you should not ignore.
I'm about to explore,
you shouldn't be here anymore.

ROAH ROAH ROAH! I'm a lion!
ROAH ROAH ROAH! Don't be frightened.
ROAH ROAH ROAH!
I'm about to explore,
and you shouldn't be here anymore.
No, you shouldn't be here anymore.

Hello I'm Melody, how are you?
Who are you, and what do you do?
I sing, dance, play and learn every day.
I've come to the zoo,
to learn fun things about you.

The
Zebras

Song

I have a thick body
and very thin legs.
A tufted tail
and a long, long head.
We are the zebras
with brilliants coats.
Black and white stripes,
we stand out the most.
(Repeat x2)

Hello I'm Melody, how are you?
Who are you, and what do you do?
I sing, dance, play and learn every day.
I've come to the zoo,
to learn fun things about you.

The Koalas

Song

I'm K K K Koala. I am very lazy,
this is my baby and he is very crazy.
His name is J J Joey,
he is nice and cosy.
We eat all the leaves,
climbing through the trees.

Then we go back to sleep
and hope there is a breeze.
(Repeat x2)

Hello I'm Melody, how are you?
Who are you, and what do you do?
I sing, dance, play and learn every day.
I've come to the zoo,
to learn fun things about you.

**The
Sloths**

I'm Sloth.
I'm
sooooooo slow
and sleeeeepppppyyyyyy
Zzzzzzzzzz

Ok, goodbye from Melody.
It's been such a wonderful day.
Maybe tomorrow we can sing, dance, play
and go on another adventure like today.

I'll see you soon,
keep smiling bright.
Until then its goodbye,
goodnight.

Kirsty Clinch is the founder
of the music school First Melodies
in Wiltshire, England.

firstmelodies.com

Music is her passion, and as
a qualified nursery nurse,
well known professional singer/songwriter and author,
Kirsty has put all her skills together to make interactive,
funny and educational music based books that co side her
YouTube channel, First Melodies.
So, you can read, have fun, and sing along with your little ones
with the help of Kirsty always.
Melody is the interactive mascot at First Melodies.

Printed in Great Britain
by Amazon

32500449R00018